THE WORK OF A
MASTER GOLDSMITH

THE WORK OF A
MASTER GOLDSMITH

A Unique Collection

JAMES MILLER

NAG PRESS

© James Miller 2009
First published in Great Britain 2009

ISBN 978 0 7198 0102 0

NAG Press
Clerkenwell House
Clerkenwell Green
London EC1R 0HT

NAG Press is an imprint of Robert Hale Limited

www.halebooks.com

A catalogue record for this book is available from the British Library

2 4 6 8 10 9 7 5 3 1

Designed by Paul Saunders

Printed in China
and arranged by New Era Printing Co. Limited, Hong Kong

CONTENTS

❧

JAMES MILLER FIPG
An English Goldsmith's Work History

J AMES MILLER is one of the many unknown craftsmen in England. Leaving secondary education at the age of fifteen in 1961, his career started with an indentured apprenticeship at one of London's major gold and silversmiths, Padgett & Braham Ltd. With workshops based in the centre of London's Soho, this company was ideally placed to supply gold and silver stock to the major West End goldsmith shops, such as Garrard and Asprey.

After a six-month probationary period, James was indentured as an apprentice goldsmith in a ceremony that took place at the Goldsmith's Hall in London. The length of the apprenticeship was set to finish on the date of his twenty-first birthday in 1967.

On his indentures, his official master was Arthur Ashfield Harvey who was a goldsmith and director of Padgett & Braham, although James was taught the trade of goldsmithing by the master goldsmith, Herbert James Jones, who was the workshop manager of the Insignia Department of Padgett & Braham. This workshop was staffed by ex-Garrard craftsmen.

Charles Stanley Padgett had taken over the whole Insignia Department from Garrard when they closed their Albemarle Street workshops in 1952. Garrard had moved premises from Albemarle Street to Regent Street, and this was when Garrard incorporated with the Goldsmiths & Silversmiths Company. This was also the year before the coronation of Queen Elizabeth II.

Herbert James Jones was the goldsmith who made the armills (amulets) that were a gift from the Commonwealth Nations to the Queen; these were commissioned from Garrard and presented to Her Majesty on the occasion of her coronation. These armills are now in the Crown Jewels display at the Tower of London.

Therefore James had the opportunity to start learning his trade from some of the best craftsmen in London at that time. The Insignia Department manufactured regalia, mainly for Garrard in the early years, and these included various orders and decorations of the British Empire.

In his time, James has made regalia for the Most Noble Order of the Garter, the Most Ancient and Most Noble Order of the Thistle, the Most Honourable Order of the Bath, the Most Distinguished Order of Saint Michael and Saint George, and sections of the Most Excellent Order of the British Empire, orders that include GBE, KBE, DBE and CBE. The department also made Field Marshals' batons, Queen's Messenger badges and various other parliamentary regalia.

James and his department also made civic regalia for the Mayors and Mayoresses of various London Boroughs and Rural Councils, mostly designed by Alex Styles of Garrard; James himself also made regalia for some American universities and societies.

In addition, the Insignia Department made regalia sets for many different countries, including Abu Dhabi, Malaysia, Bahrain, Oman, the United Arab Emirates, Libya, Canada and Jordan.

James made a Black Rod for the Parliament of New South Wales in Australia. This was a replica of the British Parliament Black Rod, with design alterations such as the crest of the New South Wales Parliament and decorations on the mounts. These design alterations were by Alex Styles of Garrard.

Padgett & Braham, where James spent the first fifteen years of his career, shared premises and workshops with Wakely & Wheeler, the silversmiths, the Flutemakers Guild, and W. Pairpoint & Son – all companies owned by Charles Stanley Padgett and situated in the same premises.

The buildings that were numbered 48 and 50 Broadwick Street, Soho, London, housed the offices, showrooms and various workshops of the group of companies.

Charles Stanley Padgett had managed to attract craftsmen from many sections of the trade, and in the London workshops there were goldsmiths, silversmiths, antique restoration silversmiths, silver-box makers, precious-metal flute makers, an engine turner, metal spinners, metal polishers and electro-platers.

The top floor of the building was occupied by the workshops of T&A Wise, a company of hand engravers, and the Insignia Department workshops were on the second floor, just below the engravers. At its peak, this collection of craftsmen in Broadwick Street would have taught over twenty indentured apprentices at any one time, with each apprentice being at different stages in his indentures. Working within this collection of companies was the start of many a successful craftsman's career.

Before completing his apprenticeship in 1967, as an indentured apprentice James was required to make his so-called 'Masterpiece' to demonstrate the skills he had attained during his apprenticeship. The designer and engraver Theodore Wise offered James one of his old designs to use for his Masterpiece. It was a design for a badge intended for the National Association of Goldsmiths that he had prepared as an unsuccessful commission. This was a perfect choice to show the level of skills that James had achieved throughout his apprenticeship.

The badge was made from silver, entirely by hand, and took James three months to complete. When it was finished, it was shown to the Wardens of the Goldsmith's Company at the ceremony when James was granted the Freedom of the Worshipful Company of Goldsmiths on completion of his indentured apprenticeship.

Once a Freeman of a liveried London company, James was also granted his Freedom of the City of London at another ceremony held at the London Guildhall.

He worked at Padgett & Braham for a further nine years after finishing his apprenticeship, and during this time he trained two apprentices as goldsmiths – a process that made him a 'Master Goldsmith'. When his former tutor, Herbert James Jones, retired in 1970, James was promoted to the position of workshop manager of the Insignia Department. In this role, he often dealt directly with the then Crown Jeweller at Garrard, William Hamilton Summers.

In 1973 Padgett & Braham moved its whole workforce out of Soho, to new premises based in Shacklewell Road, Hackney. However, many of the existing craftsmen were not happy at the company's move out of the West End, and decided to leave. This relocation also severed the close ties with Garrard, and the regalia side of the business suffered.

James remained with the company for a further three years, but yearned to be back in central London, among the rest of the trade, so decided to seek new employment.

It was in August 1976 that James joined McCabe McCarty Ltd, a newly formed company of goldsmiths with a workshop based in Rosebery Avenue, near Hatton Garden. This company had been formed by David McCarty and Peter McCabe, both highly skilled craftsmen.

David McCarty is a goldsmith of the highest calibre, and Peter McCabe was a highly regarded enameller. This new company was involved in the manufacture of high-quality gold and enamelled goods, with most pieces being of a unique style and quality not produced in the UK for many years.

When James joined, it was staffed by a group of highly skilled young craftsmen – craftsmen who had been trained at one of Cartier's London workshops, Wright & Davies.

Although James was already an experienced goldsmith, working at McCabe McCarty among such talented craftsmen gave him the opportunity to expand his knowledge and learn new skills, and in the following nine years James would do some of his best work – many pieces in the style of Fabergé, such as gold and enamelled Easter eggs. At first these designs were commissions from Asprey, but after a while McCabe McCarty employed the designer Susan K. McMeekin. She produced some of their unique designs, developing ideas and suggestions from the McCabe McCarty directors. At that time, McCabe McCarty was a major supplier to Asprey of Bond Street.

After a couple of years, James was appointed workshop manager and, as commissions increased, the McCabe McCarty workshop moved into bigger premises based in Farringdon Road. With larger workshops in the new premises, the company was able to expand its workforce, and the first two extra craftsmen who joined had themselves been apprenticed at Padgett & Braham's box-making department.

Having larger premises meant that the polisher Ben Vaughan and the engine turner Gerald Mayo could also join the workshop, and within a few years the McCabe McCarty workshop grew to accommodate a total of sixteen craftsmen and apprentices.

These craftsmen were encouraged to enter their finest pieces into the annual 'Goldsmiths Craft Council' competition, and the pieces submitted were of such high quality that they regularly won top awards in both the 'Small-workers' and 'Enamellers' sections. James himself won a total of twelve awards over the years in this annual competition – three awards being first prizes in the senior Smallworkers' section. (In later years, when James was an independent goldsmith, he was invited to be one of the judges for this Smallworker section in the annual competition.)

In 1985 James decided that it was time to leave McCabe McCarty in order to start his own workshop, outside of London, with the intention of manufac-turing more of his own designs; and his sole trading company – 'James Miller Design' – was set up in August 1985. At first he was making the unique pieces designed by Susan K. McMeekin, commissioned by his previous employer, David McCarty.

As his reputation grew, James started designing and manufacturing his own unique pieces, including the first of his enamelled gold flowers; in these, each life-size bloom, in the style of the famed Fabergé flowers, was set in specially carved rock crystal vases. James's first few flowers were purchased by David McCarty who liked his designs, and he commissioned a further four flowers from his designs.

In 1985, James was made a Fellow of the Institute of Professional Gold-smiths, and in 1986 he was commissioned to make a flower by Arthur Withers, himself an ex-Cartier craftsman. Arthur was working on a commission from Cartier and required James's flower-making skills to make a golden rose to dec-orate the top of a casket he was making. In the process of this collaboration, after a joint visit to the Cartier design studio in Bond Street, Arthur Withers invited James to accompany him on a visit to another of his customers, Gerald Earle and Peter Stein, directors of Sannitt & Stein Ltd, a company who made and supplied jewellery and watches to Kutchinsky of Knightsbridge.

Gerald Earle was seeking a goldsmith who could manufacture and supply them with larger unique pieces of gold objets d'art, similar to the style of pieces that McCabe McCarty was making for Asprey.

At first James was commissioned by Sannitt & Stein to make some items designed by the Kutchinsky design team. These included a mystery clock; a pair of large rock crystal photo frames; a pair of amethyst bowls supported by ornate bases, and a matching, thirty-inch high pair of egg-shaped flower baskets, incorporating various carved stone flowers set in an ornate egg-shaped rock crystal basket – a design that was loosely based on the nine-inch high Fabergé 'basket of flowers' egg.

On completion of the Kutchinsky orders, James was invited by Gerald Earle to design an Easter egg. He duly prepared some designs and his one for 'the Flax egg' was accepted and commissioned by Kutchinsky. This was to be the start of a long business relationship with the partners of Sannitt & Stein, Gerald Earle and Peter Stein.

Gerald Earle and Peter Stein then started a new company called Carelle to market the new designs and items of precious-metals objets d'art on to other trade customers such as Asprey and Garrard. Sannitt & Stein eventually ceased trading, and in 1996 Carelle moved to new premises before themselves ceasing to trade.

Gerald Earle and his partner Peter Stein dissolved their partnership in 1997, but James continued his working relationship with Gerald Earle who was now marketing goods in his own name. Together, James and Gerald designed a range of table centrepieces, some of which were sold, via agents, to the family of the Sultan of Brunei as palace table decorations. James also manufactured occasional items for Gerald Earle until Gerald's retirement in 2006.

James also worked with another talented designer jeweller, Edward D. Evans, and over the period 1988 to 1999 they created some of Edward Evans's unique designs – mainly supplying Asprey once again. Most of these pieces were commissioned by the Brunei royal family for use as decoration in the houses and royal palace of the Sultan of Brunei.

James is a hand-crafting, bench-working goldsmith – which means that he uses techniques that have changed very little over the centuries. He manufactures the metalwork designs from gold and silver, starting from a stock of flat sheet and wires, and forms the finished shapes using a hand saw, various shaped hammers, gravers and files. Many separate pieces are shaped to complete the finished designs.

In order to produce work of the finest quality, James insists on adding the skills of the best specialist craftsmen to his work – including silversmith metal spinner Stefan Coe, who spins the basic shapes used on his larger circular designs. James adds colour to his pieces using the craftsmanship of enamelling companies such as Kempson & Mauger and Alan Mudd Partnership; these include the skills of the craftsmen enamellers Graham Hamilton, Clive Penney, Alan Mudd, Keith Seldon and Simon Evans. This enamelling is high-quality kiln-fired enamels – techniques similar to those used by the craftsmen in the Fabergé workshops. Beneath some of the transparent enamelling is a patterning technique called engine turning; after enamelling, this technique is sometimes known as guilloche work.

The engine turning on James's work was mostly achieved by the skills of Gerald Mayo, using his hand-operated Plant engine turning machines. Gerald is another ex-Wright and Davies, Cartier craftsman.

Complicated hand engraving, when required, was achieved by various craftsmen engravers – men such as George Lukes, Peter McCabe, Steve Munro and Larry O'Connell.

The simple engraving and outlining tasks were done by James himself. Outlining was the method used to engrave the design patterns on to the metal surface before saw piercing or carving, with fine hand-saw piercing being one of James's special skills and used on most of his finest work.

No one craftsman can be expected to master all the skills involved in producing such high-quality objects, so James still chooses to use the additional skills of the best craftsmen in certain aspects of his trade – the precious stone setters, the lapidaries and various metal polishers and presentation case makers. These are all craftsmen in their own fields, whose expertise is needed to produce a finished article of high quality.

The illustrations included in this book are a selection of unique gold and silver creations spanning over forty years' work of James Miller FIGG.

THE
ILLUSTRATIONS

ITEMS MADE WHILE
JAMES MILLER WAS EMPLOYED
AT PADGETT & BRAHAM
1961–76

This photo, taken in 1966, shows a section of the workbench in the Insignia Department of Padgett & Braham in Broadwick Street, Soho, London. Seated at the workbench, from the front is the workshop manager, master goldsmith Herbert James Jones, then Don Spratling, a journeyman goldsmith, and finally James Miller, the apprentice goldsmith.

The front of the Padgett & Braham, Wakely & Wheeler, Goldsmith and Silversmith's premises at 50 Broadwick Street, Soho, London, 1970.

A silver badge, made by James Miller as his 'Masterpiece' at the end of his apprenticeship. James was formally indentured as an apprentice goldsmith to his official master, Arthur Ashfield Harvey, at the Worshipful Company of Goldsmiths, and as part of the terms of his indentures he had to produce a totally hand-made Masterpiece. This piece was made to show the skills James had mastered during his apprenticeship and would be shown to the Prime Warden at his Freedom Ceremony held at the Goldsmith's Hall on completion of his indentured apprenticeship.

The badge was a design by Theodore Wise, an unsuccessful design proposal of a badge intended for the National Association of Goldsmiths. The design was kindly given to James for use as his Masterpiece design (1967).

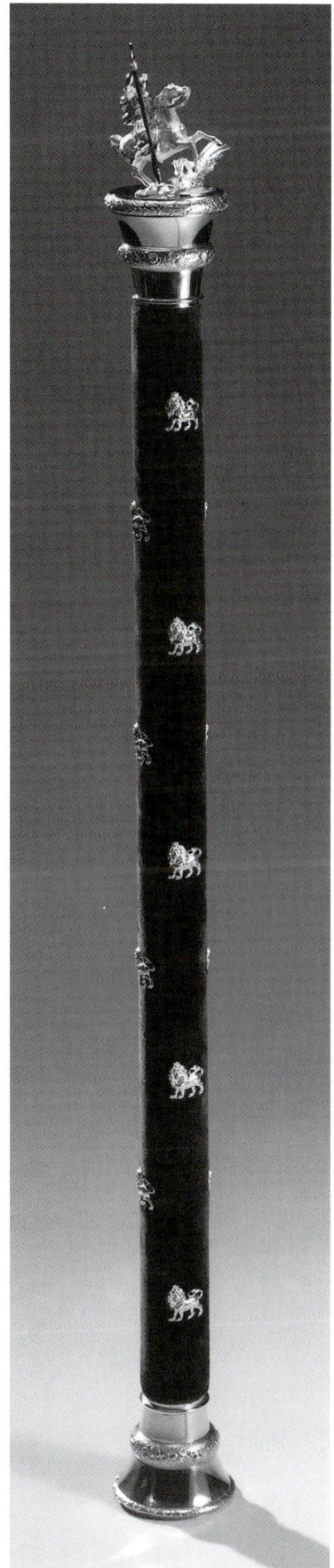

These are photos of a field marshal's baton. The mounts are made from 18ct gold; the top mount has a model of George and the dragon, while the bottom mount has the official inscription engraved on it. The two mounts are fitted to a velvet-covered baton staff which has eighteen lions fitted at regular intervals along the length of the baton.

Made for Garrard, the Crown Jeweller. Total baton length approximately 400mm (1966).

KCB star, military division, regalia also made
regularly for Garrard.

A badge for the Society of Advocates in
Aberdeen; a design by Alex Styles of Garrard,
made in 9ct gold. Badge size 80mm (1969).

A badge for the president of the Old Fettesian Association designed by Eric
Clements. The crest is that of Sir William Fettes, made from red, yellow and
white gold with silver additions. Badge size 100mm.

A badge for the President of the American Gynecological Club: a design by Alex Styles of Garrard; 18ct white and yellow gold.

Commissioned by Garrard. Badge size 80mm (1970).

A badge for the Chairman of Tiverton District Council; made in 18ct gold and enamels.

Designed by James Miller; enamelling by Kempson Mauger; a commission by the Viscount Lord Amory to Padgett & Braham for the design and manufacture of the badge. Badge size 120mm (1974).

Top and bottom mounts for a baton, commissioned by Garrard as regalia for King Idris of Libya. The baton was a design and commission by Garrard. The mounts are fitted at each end of a velvet-covered wooden shaft, with twenty-two, five-pointed stars mounted evenly along its length; 18ct gold. Total baton length approximately 400mm (1967).

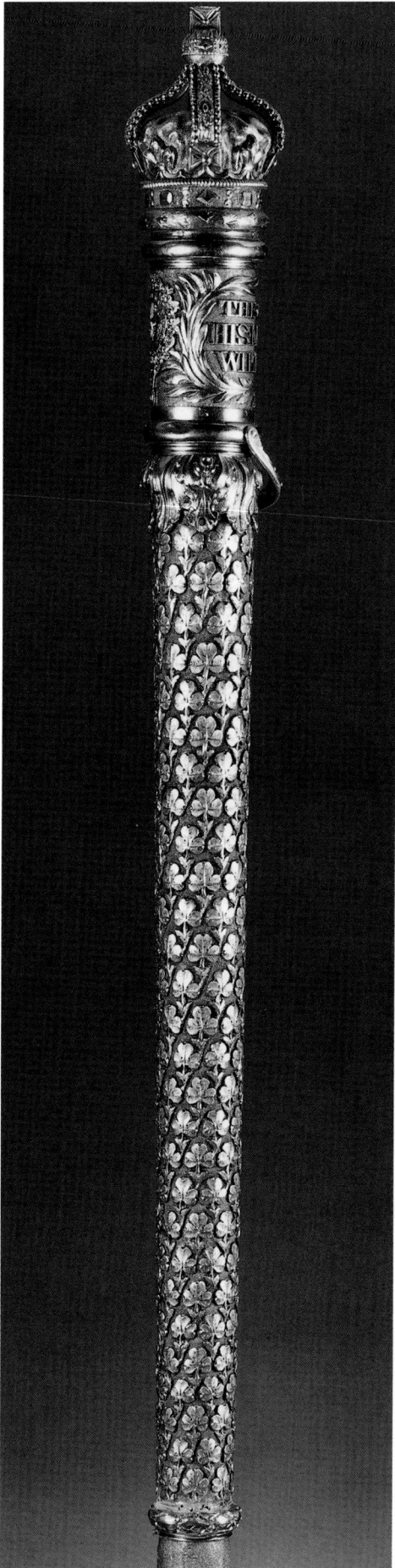

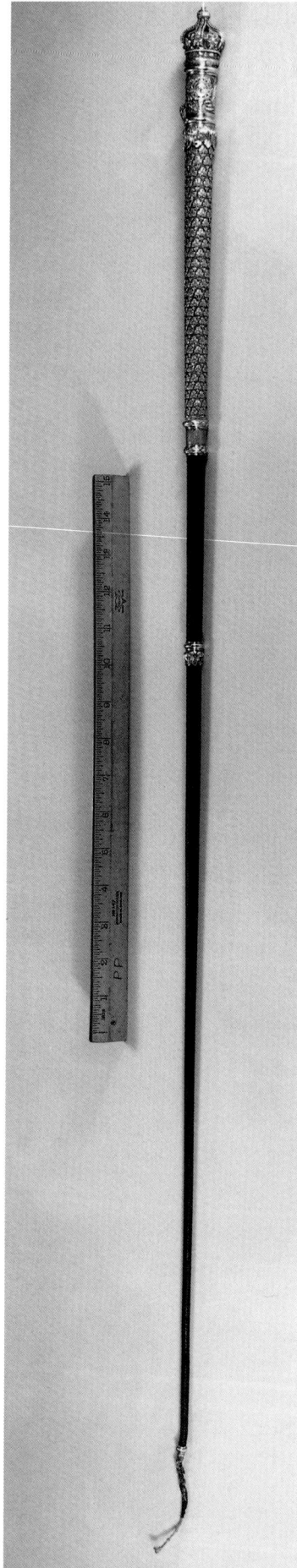

A replica of the 'Royal Whip', an Irish horse racing trophy. The original trophy whip was a gift from King William IV in 1830. This replica was made as a commission from Captain Marcus Lemus, whose horse had won the 'Royal Whip' trophy the previous year. The Captain wanted to have an identical replica to display in a showcase at his London office. The whip was made using traditional goldsmithing techniques, with each piece being cut and shaped by hand. The hand engraving was by the master engraver George Lukes. The whip mounts were made from 18ct red, yellow and green golds. The handle mount length was 300mm, and the total length of the whip was approximately 1m (1972).

Malaysian regalia, a star, badge and collar; silver gilt.

A commission from Garrard.

ITEMS MADE BY JAMES MILLER
WHILE EMPLOYED
AT McCABE McCARTY

1976–85

❧

ABOVE AND OPPOSITE PAGE An Easter egg, 18ct gold; a dragonfly with plique a–jour enamelled wings; enamelled body with a diamond-set tail is perched on the top of the egg. The egg shells are engine turned in a wave pattern and enamelled with random rush leaves. The egg itself opens centrally and sits amid a clump of enamelled bullrushes, which appear to be growing from a slice of moss agate, representing the surface of a pond; also on the moss agate surface, set alongside the rushes, is a small pink enamelled water lily flower complete with a few leaves. Inside the egg there is a surprise – a lily pond covered with four enamelled lily pads and one pink lily; on the largest lily pad sits a frog. The small lily pad next to the lily pad with the frog is a secret button – when it is pressed, a hidden watch springs up to reveal itself from beneath the large lily pad, thus creating the surprise.

Designed by James Miller; enamelling by Kempson Mauger; engine turning by Gerald Mayo. Height 160mm (1977).

Two Blue John bowls, each with 18ct gold mounts. The Blue John bowls were cut by an unknown lapidary, from a fluorite mineral variety that was mined in Derbyshire.

Engine turning by Gerald Mayo; a commission from Garrard. Heights 100mm and 70mm (1978).

A rock crystal triangular clock with an 18ct gold frame. At each angle of the rock crystal, a swag of coloured gold flowers is set. The clock movement is a mechanical eight-day movement.

A design by James Miller; clockwork by master clockmaker Paul Mason. Height 150mm (1979).

A badge for the Association of Australian Dentists; 18ct gold and enamels.

A design by, and commission from, Leo DeVroomen Jewellers; enamelling by Kempson Mauger. Length 80mm (1978).

A desk paperweight in the form of a pair of European bee eaters in flight, set on a mineral specimen of galena; 18ct gold and enamels.

A design and commission from Asprey; enamelling by Kempson Mauger. Height 200mm (1980).

A set of regalia for Jordan, Order of al-Hussain ibn Ali – established for award to foreign heads of state in recognition of special and extraordinary honour. 18ct gold and enamels. The collar and its pendant badge are set with diamonds.

A design and commission from Garrard (1983).

The Jordanian regalia as worn by the Queen of England and Queen of Jordan. This photo is a copy from a press release.

A desk paperweight in the form of an 18ct gold dragonfly with plique a-jour enamelled wings and a diamond-set tail, seated on a mineral specimen that has a piece of tourmaline embedded in its side. This specimen is mounted on a slice of agate resembling a pond, with an 18ct gold, enamelled water lily and some rush leaves set on the agate surface.

Designed by James Miller; enamelling by Kempson Mauger. Height 150mm; width 200mm (1979).

HERE AND OPPOSITE PAGE A desk paperweight, based on the death mask of Tutankhamun. The mask is of 18ct gold, decorated with hard-fired enamels; the whole is mounted on a base of sodalite and stands 150mm tall. This item won a first prize for James Miller in the 'Smallworkers' section of the annual competition held by the 'Goldsmiths, Silversmiths and Jewellers Art Council of London, competition and exhibition of craftsmanship 1978'. The apprentice enameller Clive Penney of Kempson Mauger also won a first prize, and the Cartier Award in the enameller apprentice section, for his work enamelling this mask (1978).

A design and commission from Garrard.

A desk paperweight in the form of a quartz mineral specimen mounted on a base of rock crystal with sprays of 18ct gold, enamelled wild poppies, and 18ct gold corn growing from the base. An 18ct gold, plique a-jour enamelled and diamond-set butterfly is seated on the mineral specimen and a field mouse is feeding on a head of corn.

Enamelling by Kempson Mauger. Height 250mm (1985).

A desk paperweight in the form of a slice of petrified wood with sprays of 18ct gold flower stems with enamelled leaves, and sepals set with carved rock crystal blooms. Seated on the uppermost bloom is an 18ct gold, plique a-jour enamelled diamond-set butterfly.

Enamelling by Kempson Mauger. Height 160mm (1983).

A desk paperweight in the form of a rock crystal mineral specimen mounted on a slice of polished quartz. Sprouting from beneath the rock crystal specimen is a spray of violets with enamelled diamond-set blooms in 18ct gold. Seated on the violets are two 18ct gold, plique a-jour enamelled diamond-set butterflies.

Enamelling by Kempson Mauger. Height 200mm (1983).

A desk paperweight in the form of an 18ct gold, enamelled sunbird seated on a quartz mineral specimen, mounted on a rock crystal base with a pair of 18ct gold, enamelled miltonia-variety orchids with diamond-set stamens. The flower is set to appear to be growing from the shaped rock crystal base.

Enamelling by Kempson Mauger. Height 200mm (1985).

James Miller saw piercing the shells of the 'Forget me not' egg at his bench in the workshop of McCabe McCarty.

BELOW AND OPPOSITE PAGE Easter egg in 18ct gold: the 'Forget me not' egg. The two egg shells have a design of forget me not flowers that are saw pierced and plique a-jour enamelled; random single diamonds are set on the top shell. The surprise that fits inside the egg is an eight-day clock with a diamond-set bezel surrounding a guilloche-enamelled dial. The clock is set in an oval slice of rock crystal that is decorated with a pattern of plique a-jour enamelled forget me not flowers. The clock's rear support stand is also a saw pierced pattern of forget me not flowers, a design that mirrors the front floral design. The egg is supported by a cluster of leaves, set on a circular rock crystal base. James Miller won first prize and the George Matthey Award in 1982 for this egg in the annual competition of the Goldsmiths Craft Council of London.

Designed by Susan K. McMeekin of McCabe McCarty; enamelling by Clive Penney of Kempson Mauger; commissioned by Asprey. Height 150mm (1981).

An Easter egg in 18ct gold; the egg shells are hand pierced and plique a-jour enamelled. Fitted inside the egg is a small removable surprise desk clock. This item won first prize in the 'Smallworkers' section for James Miller at the annual competition held by the 'Goldsmiths, Silversmiths and Jewellers Art Council of London, competition and exhibition of craftmanship 1981'. Clive Penney of Kempson Mauger also won first prize for the enamelling.

Designed by James Miller.
Height 120mm (1981).

A photo frame made from a triangular slice of nephrite decorated at its angles with swags of 18ct coloured gold flowers. The central circular photo frame has an enamelled bezel.

Designed by James Miller. Height 140mm (1985).

An eight-day, skeleton movement clock; 18ct gold and rock crystal. The clock dial bezel is set with diamonds with rubies at the hours. Around the clock dial is a circular slice of rock crystal set within an 18ct gold border. The whole clock is held aloft by 18ct gold, diamond-set foliage winding around a rock crystal base. The clock has eight 18ct gold, plique a-jour enamelled diamond-set butterflies seated at various positions around the foliage.

Designed by Susan K. McMeekin; clock work by Paul Mason; enamelling by Kempson Mauger; commissioned by Asprey. Height 300mm (1984).

ABOVE AND OPPOSITE PAGE An Easter egg, the Gooseberry egg, one of a set of 'Fruit Eggs' made for Asprey. The 18ct gold egg shells are saw pierced and enamelled with opaque and plique a-jour enamels, set with diamonds on sections of the gooseberries. The egg opens centrally to reveal a surprise – a life-size, 18ct gold, enamelled gooseberry. The gooseberry opens to reveal a watch inside that has a guilloche-enamelled dial with a diamond-set bezel. The whole egg is supported by a spray of pierced leaves sprouting from a stem, and the egg support leaves and stem are set centrally on a circular carved rock crystal base.

Designed by Susan K. McMeekin; enamelling by Kempson Mauger. Total height 180mm (1982).

ABOVE AND OPPOSITE PAGE An Easter egg, the Blackberry egg, one of a set of 'Fruit Eggs' made for Asprey. The 18ct gold egg shells are saw pierced and enamelled with opaque enamels with a design of blackberry flowers and leaves. The egg opens centrally to reveal a surprise life-size blackberry, which itself opens to reveal a watch with a diamond-set dial inside. The whole egg is supported by a spray of blackberry leaves sprouting from a stem that is set centrally on a circular carved rock crystal base.

Designed by Susan K. McMeekin; enamelling by Kempson Mauger. Height 120mm (1981).

James Miller at his workbench in the workshop of McCabe McCarty, assembling the Strawberry egg (1981).

BELOW AND OPPOSITE An Easter egg, the Strawberry egg, one of a set of 'Fruit Eggs' made for Asprey. The 18ct gold egg shells are saw pierced in a design of strawberry flowers and leaves entwining a trellis; the flowers and leaves are enamelled with opaque enamels. The egg opens centrally to reveal a surprise life-size strawberry which itself opens to reveal a watch inside with a diamond-set dial. The whole egg is supported by a spray of enamelled strawberry leaves sprouting from a base of natural rock crystal.

Enamelling by Kempson Mauger. Height 200mm (1981).

HERE AND OPPOSITE PAGE An Apple surprise; a life-size 18ct gold apple seated on a spray of leaves. The apple opens vertically midway, to reveal inside an eight-day clock; a guilloche-enamelled dial is mounted in one half and a pair of enamelled oval photo frames are set in the other. A ladybird insect set between the two photo frames is a secret button that releases the photo frames to allow insertion of photographs.

The engine turning on the apple interior is by Gerald Mayo; clock work by Paul Mason; a design and commission from Asprey. Height 100mm (1981).

ABOVE AND OPPOSITE PAGE Kettle drum surprise; an 18ct gold, guilloche-enamelled miniature kettle drum. The drum sticks have heads set with diamonds, and the drum skin revolves to reveal an eight-day clock with a guilloche-enamelled dial on its reverse. The clock has diamond-set hands and a ruby-set bezel with diamonds set at the hour marks.

Enamelling by Kempson Mauger; engine turning by Gerald Mayo; clock work by Paul Mason; a commission from Garrard. Height 100mm (1983).

An oval agate bowl; 18ct gold carved leaf design. The top mount follows the natural shape of the carved agate bowl and is set with cabochon rubies at intervals; the foot mount is enamelled. Width 150mm (1982)

A table decoration in the form of a piece of azurite mounted on a slice of agate. Growing from beneath the azurite specimen are three stems of an 18ct gold flower with carved rock crystal blooms and a bud. Seated on the uppermost rock crystal bloom is an 18ct gold, enamelled dragonfly with saw pierced plique a-jour enamelled wings.

Designed by James Miller; enamelling by Kempson Mauger. Height 120mm (1983).

A desk paperweight in the form of a mineral specimen of quartz and pyrites set on a slice of petrified wood. Growing from beneath the mineral specimen is a spray of 18ct gold, enamelled wild violets with two saw pierced and plique a-jour enamelled, diamond-set butterflies seated on the flowers.

Designed by James Miller; enamelling by Kempson Mauger. Height 200mm (1981).

A table decoration in the form of a quartz mineral specimen mounted on a rectangular rock crystal base. Sprouting from the rock crystal base around the mineral specimen are 18ct gold, opaque enamelled anemones and 18ct gold sprays of corn. Seated on the anemones are two saw pierced and plique a-jour enamelled diamond-set butterflies.

Enamelling by Kempson Mauger. Height 200mm (1985).

A malachite horse head cut by the lapidary George Wilde of Idar Oberstein. The carved malachite horse head is mounted on a rectangular block of cut rock crystal. The 18ct gold, enamelled reins and head-dress were added to the sculpture. This is a design to reflect the style of decorations given to the ponies of Omani fantasy riders.

Enamelling by Kempson Mauger; a commission from Asprey. Height 200mm (1982).

An Islamic prayer mounted within a picture frame; 18ct gold, saw pierced.

Enamelling by Kempson Mauger; a commission from Asprey for the Sultan of Oman. Size 300mm square (1980).

A table decoration in the form of a slice of agate with a spray of 18ct gold flowers with enamelled leaves and two carved rock crystal blooms. A saw pierced and plique a-jour enamelled diamond-set butterfly is seated on the uppermost bloom.

Enamelling by Kempson Mauger. Height 150mm (1983).

A desk ornament in the shape of a humming bird set with rubies, emeralds and sapphires. The bird and its setting was by E. Woolf & Co. James Miller made the flowers and base mounts from 18ct gold; the bird is mounted as if in flight, feeding from one of the enamelled exotic flowers. The flowers are mounted on a slice of petrified wood. Height 200mm; petrified wood length 250mm (1983).

ABOVE AND OPPOSITE PAGE An Easter egg; the shells are of carved and faceted rock crystal, 18ct gold mounts, decorated with enamelled leaves surrounding the central egg. The egg opens to reveal its surprise, which is an 18ct gold wickerwork basket, full of enamelled diamond-set flowers. The whole egg is supported by 18ct gold vines growing from a specimen piece of white quartz mineral, decorated with random sprays of enamelled flowers.

Designed by James Miller; rock crystal egg shells by lapidary George Wilde; enamelling by Kempson Mauger. Crystal egg height 80mm; total display height 175mm (1982).

Malaysian regalia consisting of a star, a badge and a
collar with its pendant badge; 18ct gold and enamels.

Enamelling by Kempson Mauger (1981).

ITEMS MADE BY JAMES MILLER
AFTER FORMING HIS COMPANY
JAMES MILLER DESIGN
IN AUGUST 1985

A table decoration in the form of a mineral quartz specimen mounted on a slice of petrified wood. An 18ct gold strand of ivy grows from beneath the mineral specimen. This has two 18ct gold, saw pierced and plique a-jour enamelled, diamond-set butterflies seated on its stems.

Designed by James Miller; enamelling by Kempson Mauger; a commission from McCabe McCarty. Height 180mm (1985).

An 18ct gold oval photo frame, diamond-set bezel with twelve cabochon rubies set at intervals. The oval frame is mounted on a rectangular step carved rock crystal base and is cradled by a display of enamelled poppies, each with diamond-set stamens.

Designed by Susan K. McMeekin; enamelling by Kempson Mauger; a commission from McCabe McCarty. Height 180mm (1987).

ABOVE AND OPPOSITE PAGE An Easter egg, the Water lily egg. The egg shells are made from 18ct white gold and saw pierced in a lattice style, decorated with occasional enamelled lily leaves and water lily flower profiles and set with diamonds. The whole egg sits on a stand of 18ct gold, enamelled bullrushes which are growing from a carved circular rock crystal base trimmed with an 18ct gold border and three diamond-set feet. The egg opens centrally at its diamond-set mount to reveal its surprise — a removable 18ct gold, enamelled, open water lily bloom with a guilloche-enamelled dial watch set at its centre. The water lily bloom and its leaves are mounted on a rock crystal base.

Designed by Susan K. McMeekin; enamelling by Kempson Mauger; a commission from McCabe McCarty for Asprey. Height 180mm (1986).

HERE AND OPPOSITE PAGE An Easter egg, the Orchid egg; 18ct gold, saw pierced egg shells decorated with enamelled entwined paphiopedilum orchid flowers. The central hinged egg mount is diamond-set and the egg sits in a stand of entwined diamond-set leaves, mounted on a base of rock crystal. The egg opens centrally to reveal its surprise – a removable full relief model of a single paphiopedilum orchid, mounted on a small rock crystal base.

Designed by Susan K. McMeekin; enamelling by Kempson Mauger; a commission from McCabe McCarty. Height 180mm (1986).

A spray of red flowers; 18ct red and yellow golds, enamelled blooms with diamond-set stamens. All mounted in a diamond-set rock crystal vase.

Enamelling by Kempson Mauger; a commission from McCabe McCarty. Height 130mm (1987).

A spray of blue flowers; 18ct red and yellow golds, enamelled blooms with diamond-set stamens, enamelled leaves. All mounted in a rock crystal vase.

Enamelling by Kempson Mauger; a commission from McCabe McCarty. Height 150mm (1987).

ABOVE AND OPPOSITE PAGE An Easter egg, the Butterfly egg; 18ct gold egg shells, saw pierced with a design incorporating entwined grasses and plique a-jour enamelled butterfly profiles with diamond-set bodies. The whole egg is mounted on a piece of natural rock crystal and has three 18ct gold, full relief, saw pierced and plique a-jour enamelled, diamond-set butterflies settled around the egg. The egg shells open centrally at a diamond-set hinged central mount. Inside the egg is a removable surprise consisting of a small spray of diamond-set, enamelled flowers with a plique a-jour enamelled diamond-set butterfly seated on a flower bud. The flower spray is mounted on to a base of rock crystal, which is fitted with a watch that has a guilloche-enamelled dial and a diamond-set bezel.

Designed by Susan K. McMeekin; enamelling by Kempson Mauger; a commission from McCabe McCarty. Height 150mm (1983).

A silver commemorative plaque, presented to the Sultan of Oman on the twentieth anniversary of Oman. The silver gilt centre is a semi relief portrait of the Sultan of Oman, set on an oval slice of lapis lazuli which is surrounded by palm leaves. The area around the portrait has engraved scenes depicting the achievements of the State of Oman.

Engraving by Steve Munroe; a commission from McCabe McCarty. Height 700mm (1987).

A pair of cattleya orchids; 18ct gold, enamelled blooms with diamond-set stamens. The orchids are mounted in a carved rock crystal candlestick-shape vase.

Designed by James Miller; enamelling by Kempson Mauger; a commission from McCabe McCarty. Height 220mm (1987).

A camellia-type flower; 18ct gold, enamelled bloom with diamond-set stamens. An 18ct gold, plique a-jour enamelled dragonfly with a sapphire-set body is seated on a leaf. The whole flower is set into a rock crystal vase, carved to appear full of water.

A design by James Miller for Sannitt & Stein; vase by Emil Becker; enamelling by Kempson Mauger. Height 220mm (1987).

The same flower as opposite, except with a change in
bloom colour and enamel added to the leaves.

A cornflower and wild oats; 18ct gold, enamelled blooms with diamond-set stamens, with a bee mounted on one bloom. The flower and oats spray is set into a rock crystal vase, carved to appear full of water.

A design by James Miller for McCabe McCarty; lapidary by George Wilde; enamelling by Kempson Mauger. Height 180mm (1987).

A lily of the valley flower; 18ct gold stems, and enamelled leaves. The blooms are made of pearls with diamond-set mounts. The whole flower is set in a hand-blown vase.

A design by James Miller for McCabe McCarty; enamelling by Kempson Mauger; glass blowing by Norman Stuart Clarke. Height 180mm (1987).

A bud rose; 18ct gold, enamelled bloom and leaves. The flower is set in a hexagonal rock crystal vase, carved to appear full of water.

A design by James Miller for McCabe McCarty; lapidary by George Wilde; enamelling by Kempson Mauger. Height 225mm (1987).

RIGHT A pair of chrysanthemums; 18ct gold, two blooms, each enamelled a different colour, and enamelled leaves. The whole is set into a diamond-set rock crystal vase.

A design by James Miller for McCabe McCarty; enamelling by Kempson Mauger. Height 200mm (1987).

A desk paperweight in the form of an 18ct gold, diamond- and ruby-set, enamelled humming bird in flight. The bird is feeding from one of a pair of rock crystal flowers with diamond-set stamens. The flower stems and enamelled leaves are of 18ct gold and are mounted on a slice of petrified wood.

A design by James Miller for McCabe McCarty; enamelling by Kempson Mauger. Height 150mm (1988).

A single carnation and bud with a plique a–jour enamelled, diamond-set butterfly seated on the enamelled flower bloom. The whole is set in a rock crystal vase, carved to appear full of water.

A design by James Miller; enamelling by Kempson Mauger; lapidary by George Wilde; commissioned by McCabe McCarty. Height 225mm (1988).

A large carved oval fluted, rock crystal bowl, decorated with two varieties of 18ct gold, enamelled clematis flowers, each with diamond-set stamens.

A flower design by James Miller; enamelling by Kempson Mauger; commissioned by (and bowl supplied by) McCabe McCarty. Height 300mm (1996).

A spray of forget me not flowers; 18ct gold, enamelled blooms set
with diamonds. The whole spray is set in a rock crystal vase, carved
to appear full of water.

*A design by James Miller; enamelling by Kempson Mauger; lapidary by
George Wilde; commissioned by McCabe McCarty. Height 200mm (1987).*

A spray of blue flowers and rush leaves; 18ct gold, enamelled blooms with diamond-set stamens. The whole is set into a rock crystal vase, carved to appear full of water.

A design by James Miller; enamelling by Kempson Mauger; commissioned by McCabe McCarty. Height 250mm (1988).

A pair of yellow chrysanthemums; 18ct gold, with enamelled blooms. The whole is set in a rock crystal vase, carved to appear full of water.

A design by James Miller; enamelling by Kempson Mauger; commissioned by McCabe McCarty. Height 220mm (1988).

A golden rose, silver gilt.

A commission from Arthur Withers, part of an original design and commission from Cartier. Length 200mm (1986).

A wildflower spray in 18ct gold, consisting of two corncockle flowers with enamelled blooms and sepals and diamond-set stamens, set alongside two seedheads of corn. A dragonfly with saw pierced and plique a-jour enamelled wings and a diamond-set body is seated on one of the corn leaves. The whole wildflower spray is set in a rock crystal vase, carved to appear full of water, by the lapidary Emil Becker.

A design by James Miller; enamelling by Kempson Mauger; commissioned by Sannitt & Stein. Height 220mm (1989).

An oval trellis-style photo frame; 18ct gold, saw pierced trellis work with a spray of enamelled diamond-set flowers adorning the trellis. The oval bezel surrounding the photo area is set with diamonds and the top oval has a profile of a plique a-jour enamelled butterfly complete with a diamond-set body.

A design by James Miller; enamelling by Kempson Mauger; commissioned by Sannitt & Stein. Height 120mm (1988).

ABOVE AND OPPOSITE PAGE A pair of amethyst fruit bowls. Carved amethyst bowls with stems made of silver, guilloche-enamelled sections overlaid with 18ct gold, saw pierced trellis work, set with diamonds at the intersections on the ball section.

A design by (and bowls supplied by) Kutchinsky; enamelled by Kempson Mauger; engine turning by Gerald Mayo; commissioned by Sannitt & Stein. Heights approximately 300mm (1989).

A bird of paradise on flowers; 18ct gold bird of paradise, diamond-set head, enamelled body with plique a-jour enamelled tail feathers. The bird is seated on the stem of a spray of flowers, 18ct gold stems and leaves, rock crystal blooms with enamelled sepals and diamond-set stamens. The whole is set in a freeform carved rock crystal base.

A design by James Miller; enamelling by Kempson Mauger; commissioned by Sannitt & Stein. Height 250mm (1991).

A pair of Arabic-style photo frames; 18ct gold framework to 10mm thick slices of rock crystal. The central oval photo frame is surrounded by a diamond-set bezel. The top mount is in the form of a diamond-set floral design overlaying a blue guilloche-enamelled background. The bottom mount is of a trellis work style with a central, heart-shaped cabochon ruby and single-set diamonds, also overlaying a pale blue guilloche-enamelled background. The rear of the frame is decorated with engine turning and the central photo frame is backed with a removable burr walnut back plate.

A design by Kutchinsky; engine turning by Gerald Mayo; enamelling by Kempson Mauger; commissioned by Sannitt & Stein. Height 300mm (1989).

OPPOSITE PAGE A mystery clock, made from 18ct gold and silver. The clock glasses are made from two 55mm diameter faceted citrines, surrounded by a diamond-set bezel with pear-shaped diamonds set at the quarters. A pale blue guilloche-enamelled plate completes the clock face. The clock is mounted on a silver guilloche-enamelled base with a diamond-set 18ct gold bezel surrounding the clock base, and 18ct gold, diamond-set leaf-shaped mounts at each of the three ebony ball feet. At one side of the clock is a stand of 18ct gold bullrushes, with each rush head set with champagne-colour diamonds. Trailing around the clock are a spray of 18ct gold, enamelled flowers; each open bloom has diamond-set centres. Seated around the clock are three 18ct gold, plique a-jour enamelled dragonflies, each with diamond-set wings and bodies.

A design by Kutchinsky; engine turning by Gerald Mayo; enamelling by Kempson Mauger; commissioned by Sannitt & Stein. The whole piece stands 400mm (1989).

A cornflower; 18ct gold, two enamelled blooms each with diamond-set stamens. The flower stems are of 18ct red gold, the enamelled blooms are of 18ct white gold, and the leaves, stamens and bud are of 18ct yellow gold. The whole is set in a rock crystal vase complete with a diamond-set mount around its base. The vase is carved from rock crystal to appear full of water.

A design by James Miller; rock crystal vase by Emil Becker; enamelling by Alan Mudd; commissioned by Carelle. Height 230mm (1989).

HERE AND OPPOSITE PAGE An Easter egg, the Flax egg; 18ct gold, the shells and base support are saw pierced and carved to a design depicting a group of standing flax flowers. The blooms and leaves are enamelled, and each bloom has a diamond set in its centre. A diamond-set ball surrounds a cluster of leaves that form the egg's support. The egg support stands on a pale blue guilloche-enamelled base complete with diamond-set mounts. The egg has a central diamond-set hinged mount which opens to reveal its removable surprise – a spherical clock that itself opens centrally to reveal a watch inside with a guilloche-enamelled dial and a diamond-set bezel. The lid section of the spherical clock is pavé-set with diamonds.

A design by James Miller; engine turning by Gerald Mayo; enamelling by Alan Mudd; commissioned by Sannitt & Stein for Kutchinsky. Height 250mm (1988).

A table decoration in the form of a humming bird, in flight feeding from a rock crystal flower. The bird is 18ct gold, enamelled and set with diamonds on its face and wings; cabochon emeralds are set as eyes. The flower stems are of 18ct red gold and the leaves are of 18ct yellow gold. The blooms are carved rock crystal, each with diamond-set stamens. The flower group grows from a pyromorphite mineral specimen mounted on a turned rosewood base.

A design by James Miller; enamelling by Alan Mudd; commissioned by Carelle. Height 200mm (1989).

Lily of the valley flower; 18ct red gold stems, pearl-set blooms with diamond-set mounts beneath most pearls. The leaves are enamelled 18ct yellow gold, and the whole flower is set in a rock crystal vase complete with an 18ct gold mount around its base. The rock crystal vase is carved to appear full of water.

A design by James Miller; enamelling by Alan Mudd; rock crystal vase by Emil Becker; commissioned by Carelle. Height 200mm (1990).

A single chrysanthemum; 18ct gold, enamelled bloom and leaves, a small diamond-set insect is seated on the bloom. The whole is set in a rock crystal vase with a diamond-set bezel around its top edge. The rock crystal vase is carved to appear full of water.

A design by James Miller; enamelling by Kempson Mauger; rock crystal vase by Emil Becker; commissioned by Carelle. Height 200mm (1990).

A head of hydrangea; 18ct gold, enamelled blooms, each bloom with a cabochon sapphire set at its centre. Three 18ct gold, enamelled leaves at the base of the stem. The whole is set in a rock crystal vase, carved to appear full of water.

A design by James Miller; enamelling by Alan Mudd; rock crystal vase by Emil Becker; commissioned by Carelle. Height 250mm (1991).

A spray of wild poppies; 18ct gold, enamelled blooms with diamond-set stamens, 18ct red gold stems and 18ct yellow gold, enamelled blooms and leaves. The whole flower spray is set in a rock crystal vase, carved to appear full of water.

A design by Gerald Earle; enamelling by Alan Mudd; rock crystal vase by Emil Becker; commissioned by Carelle. Height 250mm (1988).

OPPOSITE PAGE An oval trellis clock; 18ct gold, oval saw pierced trellis design clock with an enamelled dial surrounded by an oval diamond-set bezel. The clock stands on a rock crystal base with a stand of wildflowers at its side. The wildflowers are 18ct gold with transparent pink enamelled blooms, each with a cluster of diamond-set stamens.

A design by James Miller; enamelling by Alan Mudd; commissioned by Carelle. Height 250mm (1991).

HERE AND OPPOSITE PAGE A letter
opener, 18ct white gold blade with an
18ct yellow gold pommel. The pommel is
pavé-set with diamonds, and the letter
opener handle is leather covered. The
pommel opens centrally to reveal a watch
inside that has a guilloche-enamelled dial
surrounded by a diamond-set bezel. At the
top centre of the pommel, set amid the
diamonds, there is a monogram made up of
set rubies. The monogram letters are J B.
This item was for Prince Jefri Bolkiah of
Brunei, the younger brother of the Sultan
of Brunei.

*A design by James Miller; enamelling by Alan
Mudd; commissioned by Carelle for Asprey.
Length 260mm (1991).*

A pelargonium flower head; 18ct gold, ten enamelled blooms with diamond and ruby-set centres. There are clusters of 18ct gold buds on a side shoot and three enamelled leaves at the base of the 18ct red gold flower stem. The whole flower is set in a rock crystal vase, carved to appear full of water; around the foot of the vase is a plain 18ct gold mount.

A design by James Miller; enamelling by Alan Mudd; rock crystal vase by Emil Becker; commissioned by Carelle. Height 250mm (1991).

A single rose with trailing ivy; 18ct gold, the rose has an enamelled bloom and leaves; the bloom's central petal tips are set with diamonds to appear tipped with frost. A plique a-jour enamelled butterfly with a diamond-set body sits on one of the 18ct yellow gold trailing ivy leaves. The whole flower group is set in a rock crystal vase, carved to appear full of water.

A design by James Miller; enamelling by Alan Mudd; rock crystal vase by Emil Becker; commissioned by Carelle. Height 200mm (1992).

An Islamic prayer; an oval slice of rock crystal holds an oval enamelled prayer at its centre. The prayer is surrounded by an 18ct gold, diamond-set bezel. The oval rock crystal frame and prayer are mounted on a silver guilloche-enamelled base complete with three 18ct gold and ebony feet. The prayer is cradled by a cluster of 18ct gold, yellow-enamelled poppies, each bloom with diamond-set stamens; behind the poppies is a stand of three heads of corn with enamelled leaves.

A design by James Miller; rock crystal by Emil Becker; enamelling by Alan Mudd; engine turning by Gerald Mayo; commissioned by Carelle. Height 300mm (1993).

OPPOSITE PAGE A table centre decoration consisting of a pot-pourri bowl mounted on a silver guilloche-enamelled base and cradled by 18ct gold, enamelled poppies, each with diamond-set stamens. At the base of the poppies is a spray of enamelled trailing ivy. The pot pourri bowl has a silver guilloche-enamelled bowl with an 18ct gold, saw pierced overlay and an 18ct gold, saw pierced lid, set with diamonds around the button mount.

A design by James Miller; engine turning by Gerald Mayo; enamelling by Alan Mudd; commissioned by Carelle. Height 250mm (1997).

A single orchid; 18ct gold, enamelled bloom with a diamond-set stamen, enamelled leaves. On a leaf sits a saw pierced and plique a-jour enamelled butterfly with a diamond-set body. The whole piece is set in a rock crystal vase, carved to appear full of water.

A design by James Miller, with enamelling by Simon Evans, apprentice to the craftsman enameller Keith Seldon of Alan Mudd partners, this piece was used as Simon's 'Masterpiece' at the end of his indentured apprenticeship; rock crystal vase by Emil Becker. Height 200mm (1991).

Table centre set No 1; a tall stand with central flowers and three bowls mounted around its central stand. There are also three satellite bowls, each with three rock crystal ball feet; each bowl has 18ct gold, saw pierced overlays on pale blue silver guilloche-enamelling. The central support stand also has 18ct gold pierced overlays. The top bowl is filled with seventeen 18ct gold, pink enamelled flowers, each bloom having diamond-set stamens.

An original design idea by Gerald Earle complemented by additional design ideas by James Miller; metal spinning by Stefan Coe; engine turning by Gerald Mayo; enamelling by Alan Mudd; commissioned by Carelle. Height 400mm (1994).

ABOVE AND OPPOSITE PAGE Table centre set No 2; a tall stand with central flowers and three bowls. There is also a pair of chalice-style bowls making up this set, each with 18ct gold, saw pierced overlays over blue silver, guilloche-enamelled. The central stand also has 18ct gold, saw pierced overlays on blue silver guilloche-enamelled bowls and central stand. The top bowl is filled with 18ct gold, yellow enamelled flowers, each bloom having diamond-set stamens.

An original design idea by Gerald Earle complemented by additional design ideas by James Miller; metal spinning by Stefan Coe; engine turning by Gerald Mayo; enamelling by Alan Mudd; commissioned by Carelle. Height 400mm (1995).

ABOVE AND OPPOSITE PAGE Table centre set No 3; a seven-bowl table centre set.
The central bowl is 400mm diameter and the six side bowls are 180mm diameter. The
bowls are engine-turned silver gilt, and each bowl is set off centre in a base of blue
guilloche-enamelled bases. The central bowl has a bouquet of 18ct gold, enamelled
flowers, each with diamond-set stamens, mounted on an engine-turned base of 18ct
white gold. The six side bowls each have a spray of 18ct yellow enamelled flowers,
each with diamond-set stamens, mounted on an engine-turned base of 18ct white
gold, itself mounted on a pale blue, silver guilloche-enamelled base.

*A design by James Miller in collaboration with Gerald Earle; metal spinning by Stefan Coe;
engine turning by David Pledge; enamelling by Alan Mudd; commissioned by Carelle (1996).*

ABOVE, OPPOSITE PAGE AND OVERLEAF Table centre set No 4; the central stand has six
bowls set around its central stem. The centre stand has a growth of thirty-five flowers at its
peak. Beside the central stand are two triple-bowl satellites. The flowers on the central stand
and those at the centre of each triple bowl are 18ct gold enamelled blooms, each with
diamond-set stamens. The central stand, its bowls and the two satellite bowl sets each have
18ct white gold, saw pierced overlays over blue guilloche-enamelled silver bowls. The central
stand is also made in the same way.

*A design by James Miller in collaboration with Gerald Earle; metal spinning by Stefan Coe; engine
turning by Gerald Mayo; enamelling by John Zeeuw; commissioned by Carelle. Height 400mm (1996).*

OPPOSITE PAGE AND OVERLEAF Table centre set No 5; the central stand has three bowls set around its central stem. The top centre bowl is of rock crystal with an 18ct gold saw pierced lid. The lid has a diamond-set button. Between each bowl is a rock crystal vase, each containing a bunch of 18ct gold, enamelled flowers with diamond-set stamens. The silver blue guilloche-enamelled bowls and central stem are fitted with 18ct gold, saw pierced scroll patterned overlays.

A design by James Miller in collaboration with Gerald Earle; metal spinning by Stefan Coe; engine turning by Gerald Mayo; rock crystal by Emil Becker; enamelling by John Zeeuw; commissioned by Carelle. Height 400mm (1998).

ABOVE AND OVERLEAF Table centre No 6; the central stand has a silver guilloche-enamelled base with an off-centre bowl and a spray of 18ct gold, enamelled flowers behind the bowl. Each bloom has diamond-set stamens. The bowls are each overlaid with 18ct gold saw piercings. The two side bowls have rock crystal ball feet.

A design by James Miller in collaboration with Gerald Earle; metal spinning by Stefan Coe; engine turning by Gerald Mayo; enamelling by John Zeeuw; commissioned by Carelle. Height 300mm (1999).

Table centre set No 7; three bowls surround a central stand of flowers displayed in three conical guilloche-enamelled vases, mounted around the central handle. The bowls and central stand are of silver and have parts guilloche-enamelled and gilt. The three saw pierced bowl lids are of 18ct gold, with rock crystal buttons set on 18ct gold, guilloche-enamelled mounts. The flowers are 18ct gold, with each bloom enamelled with diamond-set stamens set in the three conical, silver guilloche-enamelled vases. The handle has a large rock crystal sphere set at its top centre.

A design by James Miller in collaboration with Gerald Earle; metal spinning by Stefan Coe; engine turning by Gerald Mayo; enamelling by John Zeeuw; commissioned by Carelle. Height 300mm (2000).

ABOVE AND OPPOSITE Table centre set No 8; a matching pair of triple bowls, the bowls are silver guilloche-enamelled and each is overlaid with 18ct gold saw piercings. At the centre of each set of bowls is a stand of 18ct gold, enamelled flowers, each with diamond-set stamens. The flowers surround a three-arm central handle.

A design by James Miller; metal spinning by Stefan Coe; engine turning by Gerald Mayo; enamelling by Alan Mudd; commissioned by Carelle. Height 250mm (1999).

A table decoration; 18ct gold
supports hold a pair of rock crystal
conical vases, carved to appear full of
water, above a rock crystal base. Each
vase is supported by a saw pierced
conical mount and both vases have a
spray of 18ct gold, enamelled flowers,
each with diamond-set stamens.
A smaller 18ct gold, enamelled
climbing flower wraps itself around
the organic vase support stems,
which themselves sprout from a
rock crystal base.

*A design by Gerald Earle and James
Miller; rock crystal by Emil Becker;
enamelling by Kempson Mauger;
commissioned by Carelle. Height
350mm (1994).*

A table decoration to complement the design opposite, an 18ct gold support holds a single rock crystal vase, carved to appear full of water, above a rock crystal base. The vase holds a spray of 18ct gold, yellow-enamelled flowers, each with diamond-set stamens. An oval trellis-style clock, with a white gold dial and a diamond-set bezel is mounted on the rock crystal base alongside the stem that supports the vase of flowers. The clock is cradled by a spray of smaller 18ct gold, enamelled flowers.

A design by Gerald Earle and James Miller; rock crystal by Emil Becker; enamelling by Kempson Mauger; commissioned by Carelle. Height 300mm (1995).

A pair of flower baskets; a design by Kutchinsky based on the Fabergé 'basket of flowers egg'. The baskets and base sections are of rock crystal; 18ct gold, diamond-set pierced overlays are set over the rock crystal egg-shape baskets and also the guilloche-enamelled base cones. The flowers are cut from various hard stones. The basket handles, flower stems and grasses are of silver gilt.

Lapidary by George Wilde of Emil Becker; a commission from Sannitt & Stein for Kutchinsky. Height 750mm (1990).

A cufflinks bowl; a guilloche-enamelled silver base, with a silver gilt bowl set off centre. Mounted at the rear of the bowl is an 18ct gold spray of enamelled flowers, each bloom having diamond-set stamens.

A design by James Miller; metal spinning by Stefan Coe; engine turning by Gerald Mayo; enamelling by Alan Mudd; commissioned by Carelle. Diameter 200mm (1996).

A silver gilt photo frame; a pale blue guilloche-enamelled base supports a circular silver gilt photo frame. Beside the frame is a stand of silver gilt, enamelled poppies, each with sapphire-set stamens. A sprig of silver enamelled trailing ivy sprouts from the base of the poppies and cradles the photo frame.

A design by James Miller; metal spinning by Stefan Coe; engine turning by Gerald Mayo; enamelling by Alan Mudd; commissioned by Gerald Earle as his gift to the 'Noah's Ark' children's cancer charity auction. Height 200mm (1998).

A posy of flowers in a rock crystal vase; 18ct gold, enamelled flowers and leaves. The blooms have diamond-set stamens and the whole is set in a rock crystal vase, carved to appear full of water.

A design by James Miller; rock crystal vase by Emil Becker; enamelling by Alan Mudd; commissioned by Gerald Earle. Height 200mm (2000).

A cornflower with trailing ivy; 18ct gold, enamelled blooms and ivy leaves. The blooms have diamond-set stamens. The flower is set in a rock crystal vase, carved to appear full of water, and is mounted on a blue guilloche-enamelled base trimmed with 18ct gold mounts.

A design by James Miller; metal spinning by Stefan Coe; engine turning by Gerald Mayo; enamelling by Alan Mudd; commissioned by Gerald Earle. Height 250mm (1999).

ABOVE AND OVERLEAF A set of three sweet bowls; the bowls are of silver gilt and are guilloche-enamelled blue, each with three rock crystal ball feet. The lids are of 18ct gold with a saw pierced design, and each lid has a guilloche-enamelled mount at its centre which is topped with a rock crystal ball.

A design by James Miller; metal spinning by Stefan Coe; engine turning by Gerald Mayo; enamelling by John Zeeuw; commissioned by Gerald Earle. Bowl diameters 150mm (2005).

A jasper-handled ebony walking cane. The cane's handle is a pale green, the guilloche-enamelled tube is complete with 18ct gold green and yellow gold carved leaf pattern mounts.

A design by James Miller for a private customer; engine turning by Gerald Mayo; enamelling by Alan Mudd; lapidary by Emil Becker. Handle length 130mm; cane length 800mm (1999).

A letter opener/paper knife; 18ct gold blade with a pale green
guilloche-enamelled handle with 18ct gold mounts topped with a
rock crystal sphere pommel.

*A design by James Miller; engine turning by Gerald Mayo; enamelling by
Alan Mudd; commissioned by Gerald Earle. Length 250mm (2000).*

A letter opener/paper knife; 18ct gold blade with a pale green guilloche-enamelled handle with 18ct green gold carved leaf mounts, topped with a rock crystal sphere pommel set in a saw pierced cup mount.

A design by James Miller; engine turning by Gerald Mayo; enamelling by Alan Mudd. Length 250mm (2001).

A letter opener to match the jasper-handled cane (page 139); 18ct gold blade with a pale green, guilloche-enamelled handle and 18ct gold green and yellow gold carved leaf mounts, topped with a jasper pommel.

A design by James Miller for a private customer; engine turning by Gerald Mayo; enamelling by Alan Mudd; lapidary by Emil Becker. Length 250mm (2001).

OPPOSITE PAGE A dog rose flower (Rosa canina); 18ct red gold stems, 18ct yellow gold, enamelled blooms and leaves. The whole flower is set in a hand-blown glass vase.

A design by James Miller commissioned by a private customer; glass vase hand blown by Siddy Langley; enamelling by Keith Seldon. Height 200mm (2003).

ABOVE AND OPPOSITE A walking cane with a puma handle; a silver gilt model puma, with ruby-set eyes, is climbing over a blue guilloche-enamelled handle with silver gilt mounts. The cane is of rosewood and is 800mm long.

A design by James Miller for a private customer; engine turning by Gerald Mayo; enamelling by Alan Mudd; wax modelling of the puma by Mary Dean. Handle length 30mm (1999).

A pair of opal white chrysanthemums with trailing ivy; 18ct red gold stems with 18ct yellow gold, enamelled blooms and ivy leaves. The whole arrangement is set in a rock crystal vase, carved to appear full of water. The vase is mounted on a pale green, guilloche-enamelled base trimmed with 18ct yellow gold mounts.

A design by James Miller; engine turning by Gerald Mayo; enamelling by Alan Mudd and Keith Seldon; rock crystal vase by Emil Becker Lapidaries. Height 250mm (2004).

A single lily bloom; 18ct gold, enamelled flower with diamond-set stamens.
The flower bloom is set in a rock crystal vase, carved to appear full of water.

*A design by James Miller; enamelling by Clive Penney; commissioned by Clive
Penney. Height 120mm (1996).*

Table centre set No 9; a silver, blue guilloche-enamelled stand, with 18ct gold, saw pierced overlays. At its centre are three 18ct gold pierced cups, holding three removable rock crystal bowls. At the top centre is a spray of 18ct gold, enamelled flowers, each with sapphire-set stamens. Seated on these central blooms are two saw pierced and plique a-jour enamelled butterflies, each with diamond-set bodies. Mounted between the three rock crystal bowls are three conical, guilloche-enamelled vases, each holding a spray of 18ct gold, enamelled flowers with stamens set with sapphires.

A design by Gerald Earle and James Miller; metal spinning by Stefan Coe; engine turning by Gerald Mayo; commissioned by Gerald Earle for a private customer. Height 350mm (2001).

An armorial brooch; 18ct gold.

*A design and commission by Alan Mudd;
enamelling by Alan Mudd. Length 80mm (2005).*

An oval photo frame of a trellis design;
18ct gold, saw pierced trellis work.
The central oval photo frame is
bordered by a diamond-set bezel. The
trellis is decorated with a profile of
enamelled flax flowers.

*A design by James Miller; commissioned
by Gerald Earle for Kutchinsky. Height
100mm (1992).*

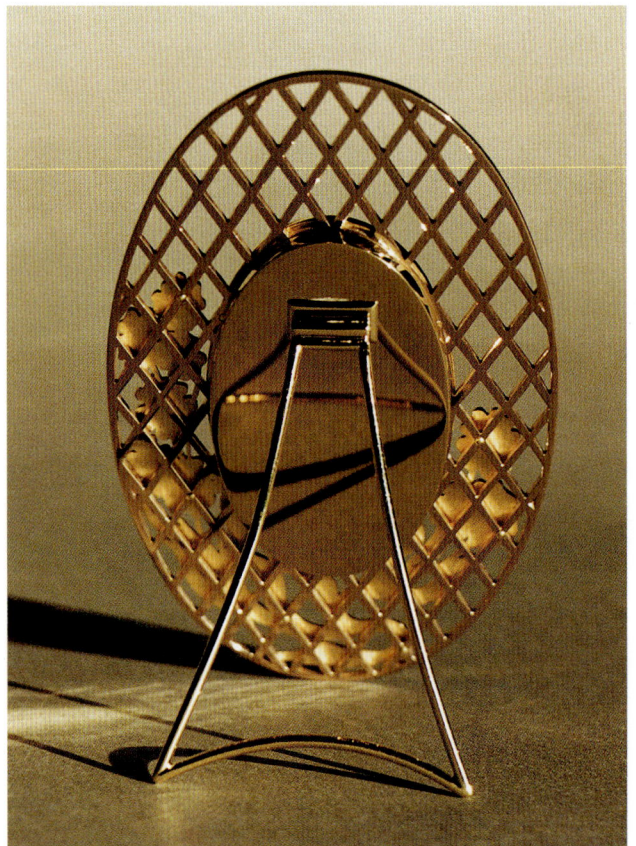

A single cattleya orchid; 18ct gold, enamelled bloom with diamond-set stamens. The whole is set in a rock crystal vase, carved to appear full of water.

A design by James Miller; enamelling by Chris Sole; commissioned by Neville Pooley. Height 250mm (1993).

A single red rose; 18ct gold with enamelled bloom and leaves. The bloom has diamonds set on the top lip of its petals, emulating morning frost. The whole flower is set in a rock crystal vase, carved to appear full of water.

A design by James Miller; enamelling by Alan Mudd; rock crystal vase by Emil Becker; commissioned by Gerald Earle. Height 175mm (1997).

A bee on a single bloom of clover; 18ct gold, enamelled bloom, bee and leaves. The flower is set in a rock crystal vase with a diamond-set top mount.

A design and commission from Jack Perry of Perry Ltd. Height 120mm (1988).

Lily of the valley flower; 18ct red gold stems with pearl blooms and diamond-set mounts beneath most pearls. The 18ct yellow gold leaves are enamelled and the flower spray is set in a rock crystal vase, carved to appear full of water.

A design by James Miller; enamelling by Alan Mudd; rock crystal vase by Emil Becker; commissioned by Gerald Earle. Height 200mm (1996).

A portrait miniature; the central round portrait is of painted enamels, and the portrait is set into a silver square frame, its faceplate is decorated with an enamelled diamond trellis pattern.

The frame and portrait were enamelled by the enamel artist Keith Seldon, who won first prize and the Cartier Award for his enamelling, at the annual Goldsmiths Craft Council Competition of 1990. A design and commission by Alan Mudd Partnership. Size 150mm square (1990).

A kingfisher clock; an 18ct gold, enamelled kingfisher, with diamond-set tail feathers, sits on a pillar of tourmaline, which rises from a base of rock crystal. Flowers entwine the tourmaline pillar; the leaves are enamelled and the blooms are of carved rock crystal with diamond-set stamens. The clock is mounted on the rock crystal base and has a guilloche-enamelled dial surrounded by a diamond-set bezel.

A design and commission from Jack Perry of Perry Ltd; enamelling by Kempson Mauger. Height 225mm (1990).

Technical Terms and Notes

All **enamelling** is hard-fired vitreous glass enamelling; this method requires grinding of fine-quality coloured enamels into powders and, after laying the enamels on to the metal surface, the enamel is fired in gas or electric kilns.

Guilloche-enamelling is a term used to describe the technique of enamelling when transparent enamels are laid and fired over a base of engine-turned pattern work, thus allowing the pattern to show through the enamel.

The **lapidary** involved in most of the cutting of stone flowers and rock crystal vases was by George Wilde of Emil Becker Lapidaries, Idar Oberstein, Germany.

Polishing of items made while James Miller was employed at McCabe McCarty was by the company polisher Ben Vaughan, and his apprentice, Stuart Farnham.

Engine turning was by Gerald Mayo, using his straight line and rotary, hand-operated Plant engine turning machines. One item was engine turned by David Pledge; this was only because the item was too large to fit on to Gerald Mayo's rotary machine.

Metal spinning is a term used for shaping round and conical shapes. The method is to turn a hard wood shape on a lathe, then metal shapes can be formed by means of spinning and forming a disc of metal over the hardwood shape on a lathe. The skills of silversmiths Henry Pierce and Stefan Coe were used for this process.

Most **gold and rhodium plating** of silver and white gold items would have been achieved by the skills of silversmith Eric Parker – first when he was at W. Pairpoint, and later at his company Parker Finishing.